Maths Medicine

School has taught many people to believe that they can't do maths. This book will restore your mathematical health and confidence (guaranteed!).

The items in this book involve many of the maths topics that you will have met at school, but you will not need specialist mathematical knowledge to solve them. The key to solving each day's item is to find a sensible meaning for the mathematical concepts involved. Give yourself plenty of time and discuss the item with someone, so you can check and refine your ideas. Don't worry if you go wrong. It's a step nearer going right.

The Maths Medicine website, at **www.mathsmed.co.uk**, shows the variety of methods that readers have used. The site is updated regularly, and you are invited to submit your methods and comments by using ⋯ ⋯g an email to **answers@mathsmed.co.uk**.

The Maths Medicine website provides ⋯ ⋯ item. There is also a brief answers s⋯

Maths Medicine ©

Published in the UK by

Dexter Graphics, PO Box 24320, London SW17 7WQ

tel: 020 8265 5791   fax: 020 8767 4319

© Dexter Graphics 1998   First Published 1998   Reprinted 1999

Design, illustrations and typesetting by Dexter Graphics
Printed in China by Nordica Printing Co (Panyu) Ltd

ISBN 0-9534035-0-5

Look out for

Mini Maths Medicine (2 weeks' supply of daily maths items in self-mail format) ISBN 0953403513
Junior Maths Medicine (3 months' supply for 7 - 11 year olds and their parents) ISBN 0953403521

Debra has these milk tokens.

She asks her milkman to exchange as many as possible of the lower value tokens for higher value tokens.

What tokens does she end up with?

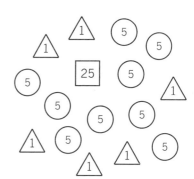

A block of butter is cut
into two identical blocks,
X and Y.

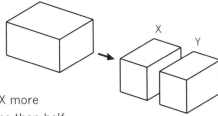

Is the total surface area of X more
than half, exactly half, or less than half
the total surface area of the original block?

Laura, Kelly and Marnie share £60.
Laura and Kelly both receive twice as
much as Marnie.

How much is Marnie's share?

All these shapes have the same perimeter, except one.

Which shape is the odd one out?

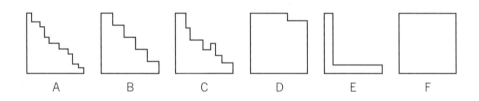

A   B   C   D   E   F

Find the cost of a large button, if

2 large buttons and 3 small buttons cost 46p, and

2 large buttons and 4 small buttons cost 54p.

Subtract 98 from 2374.

Two of these shapes are nets of a pyramid.

Which two?

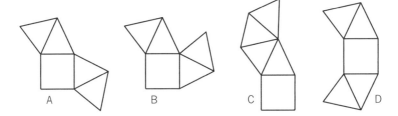

A   B   C   D

Find a fraction that lies somewhere between $\frac{1}{4}$ and $\frac{1}{5}$.

The diagonals of a kite are
4 cm and 11 cm long.

Find the area of the kite.

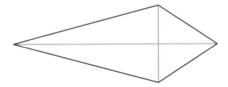

Which tastes stronger,

8 parts orange juice mixed
with 3 parts water,
or
9 parts orange juice mixed
with 4 parts water?

Lucy has £10.

Is this enough to
buy twenty eight
32p stamps?

A shape like these
has 25 white tiles.

How many blue tiles
does it have?

  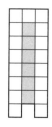

Winifred was born
on 29 February 1904
and lived till she was
90 years old.

How many of her
birthdays fell on
29 February?

A shape is made
with 1 cm cubes.
The diagram shows
the top view and
front view of
the shape.

How many cubes
are there?

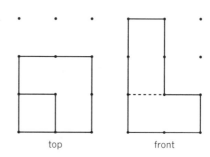

top   front

If $F \div \frac{1}{5}$ is $\frac{8}{23}$,

what is $F \div \frac{2}{5}$?

Nisha and Ben are calculating 427 × 32.

Copy and complete their calculations.

	Nisha	Ben
	427	32
	×32	×427
	12810	224
	————	————
	————	————

Which glass is most nearly full?

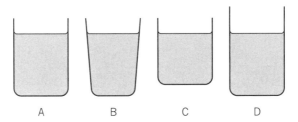

A   B   C   D

Tina buys a pen costing £8.36 with a £10 note.
The shopkeeper gives her these coins as change:

2p,   2p,   10p,   50p,   £1.

List the coins Tina might expect as change
from a £10 note for a pen costing £5.74.

This addition goes on forever:

$$P = \frac{1}{4} + \frac{1}{16} + \frac{1}{64} + \frac{1}{256} + ...$$

Use the diagram to help
you find the value of P.

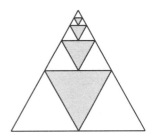

The average of

2, 3, 4, 4, 6, 8, 8, 9, 12, 16

is 7.2.

What is the average of

102, 103, 104, 104, 106, 108, 108, 109, 112, 116 ?

$21 \times 31 = 651.$

Use this to help
you calculate

$22 \times 32.$

List these in order, smallest first.

$\frac{1}{9}$ 0.9   9 %

What is the number
in row 21, column 4 ?

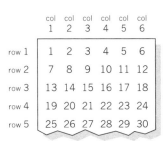

	col 1	col 2	col 3	col 4	col 5	col 6
row 1	1	2	3	4	5	6
row 2	7	8	9	10	11	12
row 3	13	14	15	16	17	18
row 4	19	20	21	22	23	24
row 5	25	26	27	28	29	30

The nail is five eighths of an inch long.

How many quarters of an inch is this?

The result of XOXX followed by XOOX is OOXO.

Find the result of XXOX followed by OXOX.

The hour hand of a clock is pointing
   to "19 minutes past the hour".

What is the minute hand pointing to?

Find the value of $r + s + r - s - r$

when $r = 4962$ and $s = 2815$.

Find the value of e when

$$\frac{24}{e + 3} = 3.$$

The table shows the numbers of telephones in the flats in Trellis Tower.

Are there more flats or more telephones?

Number of telephones	0	1	2	3	4 or more
Number of flats	2	13	23	1	0

The triangle is drawn on a 1 cm grid.

Find the area of the triangle.

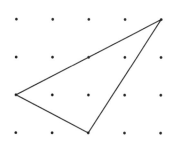

Every week a shop reduces its prices by 10 % (so the new price of any item will be 90 % of its previous price).

How long will it take for an item's original price to be halved?

10 % OFF
last week's price

$$P = 28 \times 301.$$

$$Q = 14 \times 601.$$

Without calculating P or Q, find P − Q.

Fran is covering
a concrete floor
in L·shaped
wooden tiles.

Which tile is in
the wrong place?

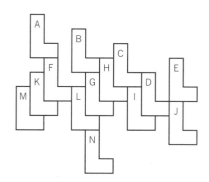

The population of a remote island has changed over the last 50 years, with the older people dying and many of the younger people leaving.

Over this period, do you think the average age of the island's inhabitants has increased, decreased, or stayed roughly the same?

The gauge shows the mileage of Ben's car.
The car is used every day.

Estimate the probability that in exactly one
year's time the mileage again ends in '85'.

◆ and ● represent single
digits in this calculation.

$$4◆3 \times 5● = 26082$$

Find the digits.

Three friends walk from their homes to the village green. The graph is for the distances walked and the times taken.

Who walked fastest?

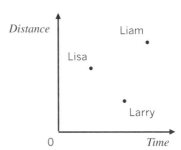

5! means $5 \times 4 \times 3 \times 2 \times 1$.

Decide which is larger, $5! \times 2$ or $(5 \times 2)!$

Sketch the 99th pattern in this sequence.

□ ◇ ⊟ ◈ □ ◇ ⊟ ◈ □ ◇ ⊟ ◈ □ ◇ ...

Grant delivers 2 full crates and 6 extra bottles of milk to the odd-numbered houses in Fox Lane. He delivers 3 full crates and 5 extra bottles to the even-numbered houses in Fox Lane.

If this is equivalent to 6 full crates and 3 extra bottles, how many bottles does a crate hold?

How many percent is 20 % of 20 % ?

The dials correctly show that 6279 units of electricity have been used. However, the pointer on one of the dials has slipped slightly.

Which dial has the loose pointer?

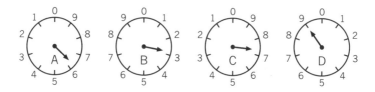

Divide $\frac{1}{5}$ by $\frac{1}{20}$.

Which sequence, P or Q,
passes 1000 more quickly?

P: 1, 6, 16, 31, 51, ...

Q: 1, 2, 4, 8, 16, ...

The drawing shows a
2 cm by 2 cm by 4 cm block.
An ant walks from corner A
to corner G.

Which is the shortest route,
ADG, ATG, AUG, AVG or ACG ?

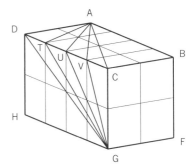

In a darts league, every team plays every other team twice (once at home, once away).

There are 10 teams. How many matches are played altogether in a season?

Gertrude Cliffe is 101.615 years old.

Approximately how old will she be
this time tomorrow?

Cara always makes toast when she gets up.
The probability that she burns the toast is $\frac{9}{10}$ when
she has overslept, and $\frac{3}{10}$ when she has not overslept.
The probability that she oversleeps is $\frac{1}{20}$.

Do you think the probability that Cara burns the toast
tomorrow is more than evens, evens, or less than evens?

ABCD is a kite.

If angle B = 80°, what is the largest size than angle A can be?

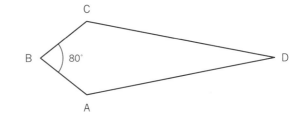

A 330 ml can of cola costs 47p.
A 333 ml bottle of the same cola costs 3p more.

Which is the better value?

Is $2\frac{1}{4} \times 3\frac{1}{7}$ less than, equal to, or greater than $6\frac{1}{28}$?

A daily spelling test is marked out of 10.
After three tests Jake's average mark is 4.

What is the maximum that Jake's average
can reach after the next test?

A to D is $2\underline{u} + 3\underline{v} - \underline{u}$,
which is $\underline{u} + 3\underline{v}$.

Write B to E in
a similar way,
as simply as
possible.

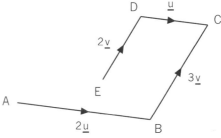

Sue goes for a walk and comes to a bus stop.
After she has waited 6 minutes, a bus arrives.

Estimate the number of buses per hour.

J is 3 km north west of P.
K is 3 km south east of P.

J is north of Q.
K is north east of Q.

How far is Q from K ?

N

W ⊕ E

S

A cubic metre of sand is
spread over part of a lawn
in a layer 1 cm thick.

How many square metres of
lawn does the sand cover?

The scores on the two spinners are added together. These are the possible totals: 2, 3, 4, 5, 6.

Is a total of 5 more likely than, equally likely as, or less likely than a total of 4 ?

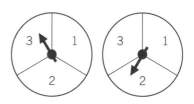

Vernon wants to share three bars of chocolate among
five people, A, B, C, D and E. He uses a process of halving.

The diagram shows the pieces that each person gets, and the
piece left over. What fraction of a bar does each person get?

Try different values for x.
Find a value for which

$$x = \frac{60}{x - 4}.$$

Two bags contain the same amount of rice.

Alan, Bjorn and Chet share the contents of one bag:
Alan gets twice as much as Bjorn who gets twice as much as Chet.

Alice, Bess and Cath share the contents of the other bag:
Alice gets five times as much as Bess who gets five times as much as Cath.

Who gets more, Bjorn or Bess?

The shape is drawn
on a 1 cm grid.

Find the area of
the shape.

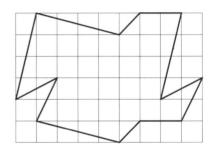

The graph shows
a cyclist's speed
for the second
lap of a race.

Roughly how long
is the race track?

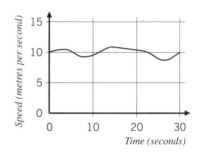

$A = 7 \times 8$ and $B = 7\frac{1}{2} \times 7\frac{1}{2}$.

How much larger is B than A ?

(You do not need to find the
actual value of B and A.)

A large floor is painted in this pattern.

What fraction of the floor is blue?

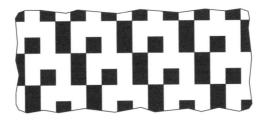

Find the values of x and y if

$x + 5y = 25$, and

$x + 6y = 28$.

0.3̈2̈ is the recurring decimal 0.32323232... .

0.3̈2̈ is equal to the vulgar fraction $\frac{32}{99}$.

(You can verify this by dividing 32 by 99 on a calculator.)

0.1̇54̇ is the recurring decimal 0.154154154154... .

Express 0.1̇54̇ as a vulgar fraction.

If the average of a, b and c is a,
what is the average of b and c ?

Henry's mileometer shows that he has travelled 284 miles on his bike.

How many more miles does he have to travel before the digits 2, 4 and 8 next appear together on the mileometer?

Which tile can be removed from this shape
without increasing or decreasing the perimeter?

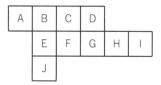

A hare and a tortoise have a race. The hare runs 10 times
faster than the tortoise but gives the tortoise a 100 metres start.

When the hare has run 100 metres, the tortoise is 10 metres ahead.
When the hare has run a further 10 metres, the tortoise is 1 metre ahead.
When the hare has run a further 1 metre, the tortoise is 0.1 metres ahead.
And so on ...

How far does the hare run before catching up with the tortoise?

Find the value
of n for which this
shape is a square.

$3n$

$n + 9$

Four pins, P, Q, R and S, are stuck
in a corkboard. An elastic band is
stretched around the pins to form
a quadrilateral PQRS.

P is moved to another position, but
without changing the area of PQRS.
Describe the possible positions of P.

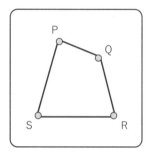

This is an "add 5, then divide by 2" sequence:

25, 15, 10, 7.5, 6.25, ...

The numbers in the sequence get smaller and smaller
but never quite reach a number, N. Find the value of N.

Ken charges 10 % more for his apples
than Linda and sells 10 % fewer.

Are Ken's takings less than, the
same as, or more than Linda's?

The arrow is pointing at 2.
When it moves on 5 places it points at 1.
So, in this system, $2 + 5 = 1$.

What do you think is the value
of 2×5 in this sytem?

Lorraine spins a coin several times.

What is the probability of the coin landing
the same way up on the 3rd and 7th spin?

Three points A (2, 2),
B (4, 3) and C (100, e)
lie on a straight line.

What is the value of e ?

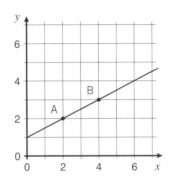

This line is 0.2 millimetres thick.

_____

How many centimetres long would the
line have to be to cover 1 cm² of paper?

The drawing shows a 6 cm cube framework, made from 1 cm cubes.

How many 1 cm cubes are needed to make a 12 cm cube framework?

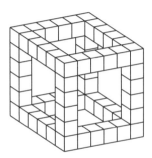

Ted takes a pill at random from one of these plates and places it on the other plate. He then takes a pill at random from this other plate and eats it.

Which plate should Ted start with if he prefers blue pills? Or does it make no difference?

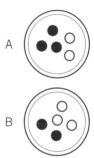

Hanif and Jenny race on their bikes
to a distant tree and back again.
Hanif cycles at 15 mph on the outward
leg and at 5 mph on the return leg.
Jenny cycles at 10 mph on the
outward and the return leg.

Does Hanif win, Jenny win, or is the race a tie?

Each apple in a fruitbowl has 6 pips.

If A stands for the number of apples in the bowl and P stands for the total number of pips, which of these represents the relationship between A and P:

$$A = 6P \quad \text{or} \quad P = 6A \text{ ?}$$

Aysha, Bob, Cherie and Dan are looking at the E shape.

Whose view looks like this?

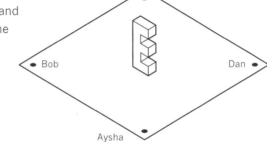

Make a sketch of this shape when its area is 17 cm².

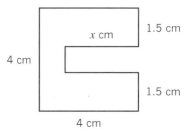

1.5 cm

x cm

4 cm

1.5 cm

4 cm

A single column of 10p coins is the same height as Mr Hodges.
Do you think there are enough coins to buy a £200 television set?

The spinner is spun twice.

Which is more likely,
getting X and then not getting X, or
getting Y and then not getting Y ?

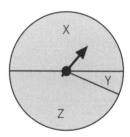

What is 110 % of 90 % ?

Varna and Sochi are on opposite
shores of the Black Sea.
Sochi is due east of Varna.

A ship sails from Varna to Sochi.
It sails due east.
Is this the shortest route?

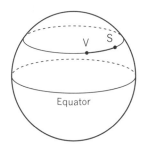

One of these graphs is for an acorn falling from a tree.
Which one?

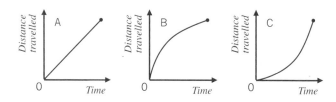

Is $\frac{1}{7}$ nearer $\frac{1}{6}$ or $\frac{1}{8}$?

DAY 32 14.   **DAY 33** E.   **DAY 34** increased.   **DAY 35** $\frac{1}{100}$.   **DAY 36** ● = 4, ◆ = 8.

DAY 37 Lisa.   **DAY 38** $(5 \times 2)!$.   **DAY 39** ⊟.   **DAY 40** 8.   **DAY 41** 4.   **DAY 42** C.   **DAY 43** 4.

DAY 44 Q.   **DAY 45** AUG.   **DAY 46** 90.   **DAY 47** about 101.618 years.   **DAY 48** less than evens.

DAY 49 140°.   **DAY 50** the can.   **DAY 51** greater.   **DAY 52** 5.5.   **DAY 53** <u>v</u> – <u>u</u>.   **DAY 54** 5.

DAY 55 6 km.   **DAY 56** 100.   **DAY 57** less likely.   **DAY 58** $\frac{19}{32}$.   **DAY 59** 10 (or ⁻6).

DAY 60 Bjorn.   **DAY 61** 35 cm².   **DAY 62** 300 m.   **DAY 63** $\frac{1}{4}$.   **DAY 64** $\frac{3}{8}$.   **DAY 65** $y = 3$ and $x = 10$.   **DAY 66** $\frac{154}{999}$.   **DAY 67** a.   **DAY 68** 144.   **DAY 69** D.   **DAY 70** 111.11… m (or $111\frac{1}{9}$ m).

DAY 71 $4\frac{1}{2}$.   **DAY 72** on a line through the original position of P, parallel to diagonal QS.   **DAY 73** 5.

DAY 74 less than.   **DAY 75** 4.   **DAY 76** $\frac{1}{2}$.   **DAY 77** 51.   **DAY 78** 50.   **DAY 79** 128.

DAY 80 B.   **DAY 81** Jenny wins.   **DAY 82** $P = 6A$.   **DAY 83** Dan's.   **DAY 84**

DAY 85 no.   **DAY 86** X then not X.   **DAY 87** 99 %.   **DAY 88** no.   **DAY 89** C.

DAY 90 $\frac{1}{8}$.   **DAY 91** it makes 2 full turns anticlockwise.   **DAY 92** 4 May 2056; day 1, year 101.

ANSWERS

These answers have been kept brief, and it is recommended that when you are working on an item you do not refer to the answer too soon. More extensive answers can be found on the Maths Medicine website, at **www.mathsmed.co.uk**. The site provides help and explanations, as well as comments and examples of methods used by readers. The site is continually updated and you are invited to submit your methods and comments using the online report form, or by sending an email to **answers@mathsmed.co.uk**.

DAY 1 25, 25, 25, 1.   **DAY 2** more.   **DAY 3** £12.   **DAY 4** C.   **DAY 5** 11p.   **DAY 6** 2276.

DAY 7 A, C.   **DAY 8** eg, $\frac{2}{9}$.   **DAY 9** 22 cm².   **DAY 10** 8 with 3.   **DAY 11** yes.   **DAY 12** 10.

DAY 13 23 (including day she was born).   **DAY 14** 6.   **DAY 15** $\frac{4}{23}$.   **DAY 16** —

Nisha	Ben
4 2 7	3 2
× 3 2	× 4 2 7
1 2 8 1 0	2 2 4
8 5 4	6 4 0
1 3 6 6 4	1 2 8 0 0
	1 3 6 6 4

DAY 17 A.   **DAY 18** eg, 1p, 5p, 20p, £2, £2.   **DAY 19** $\frac{1}{3}$.

DAY 20 107.2.   **DAY 21** 704.   **DAY 22** 9 %, $\frac{1}{9}$, 0.9.   **DAY 23** 124.

DAY 24 $2\frac{1}{2}$.   **DAY 25** XOOO.   **DAY 26** 48 minutes past.   **DAY 27** 4962.

DAY 28 5.   **DAY 29** more telephones.   **DAY 30** 4 cm².   **DAY 31** 7 weeks.

Reg Hutt was born on 4 May 1956. His followers call this date "the first day of the first year of the first century". They write it as "day 1, year 1".

What is the date of "the first day of the first year of the second century" and how do Reg Hutt's followers write it?

The cog wheels W, X, Y and Z have
30, 15, 18 and 15 teeth, respectively.

Wheel W makes 1 full turn clockwise.
What happens to wheel Z ?

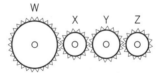